THE *Carluccio's* COLLECTION

ANTIPASTI

ANTONIO & PRISCILLA CARLUCCIO

Photography by André Martin

QUADRILLE

Contents

All recipes in the book are for 4 people unless otherwise stated. Use either all metric or all imperial measures, as the two are not necessarily interchangeable.

Foreword

Not long ago, on a visit to a small country restaurant in the province of Asti, I was presented with seven different *antipasti*, both cold and warm – one after the other, and each better than the previous one. Included in the array were Tomino (a local cheese) with parsley, garlic and chilli; crunchy celery wrapped in cured beef; prosciutto rolled in a spinach omelette; slices of fresh pear with shavings of Castelmagno cheese; *crostino* of *porcini* (cep); slices of cooking sausage with a cheese sauce and truffle; and finally a fresh salad of spinach and walnuts.

However, the meal didn't end there! After these *antipasti* I had a huge plate of immaculate home-made ravioli, followed by tagliolini pasta with cep sauce; the main course of roast beef and pheasant accompanied by braised cardoons and potatoes was also too delicious to leave, but I never got round to tasting the dessert because, as you can imagine, it was simply too much! Most importantly, the quality of the ingredients was stunning: all locally produced, from the meats to the vegetables to the truffles – and this memorable feast was a normal working man's daily lunch!

Antipasto, meaning 'before the meal', plays a very important role in the construction of an Italian meal – that of an appetizing and teasing little dish to prepare the palate and stimulate the stomach juices to greater things.

The most traditional *antipasto* consists mainly of preserved foods. Traditionally, in Emilia-Romagna, a few slices of salami, ham or other specially preserved meats, ranging from *bresaola* to *capicollo* or *coppa*, were all home-preserved and served accompanied by a few pickled foods prepared through the summer for a rainy day. The preserving was usually carried out around harvest-time, when the best crops could be utilized.

Even nowadays, in the summer, most families' kitchens are very busy producing at least a couple of jars of small onions, mixed vegetables or a little cucumber cooked in vinegar and preserved in oil. Families either use produce from their own garden or buy produce from the market to pickle at home.

The most sought-after ingredient is probably the *porcini* (cep) mushroom, which only grows wild and, whether they are self-collected or bought, are the crowning glory of a proper Northern *antipasto*. Lesser, but no less favourite, wild mushrooms like the honey fungus or chanterelle are also part of the *antipasto* scene.

Away from such classics, there is an abundance of other *antipasti* which are now more widely available. Even if families no longer produce these themselves, they are still made by those wonderful *salumerie* or delicatessens for the benefit of their customers.

Piedmont is the region with the greatest tradition of *antipasti*; there you will also find a great variety of warm *antipasto*, based on cooked items with the addition of truffles. Great *antipasti* traditions are also found in Liguria, Venice and most coastal regions. The Southern tradition of *antipasto* is based more on fish, cheese or vegetables, and takes advantage of locally grown ingredients. The absolutely unforgettable *bottarga* of mullet or tuna is largely consumed in Sardinia and Sicily, while dried or salted tuna and swordfish takes the place held by salami in the North.

Today's abundance and variety of *antipasto* dishes, which are traditionally from the North of Italy but which are now also spreading to the South, have revolutionized the way in which a Italian meal is eaten. Usually a chef prepares a meal which begins with his choice of *antipasto* and this is followed by a first course, a main course, along with salad, cheese and dessert, according to the occasion. This is normally what we Italians eat, but the portions are therefore small, and the content is varied to avoid overfilling the stomach. The quantities of fats, proteins, starch and liquids alternate, thereby providing the perfect dietary balance. Due to today's greater variety of *antipasti*, however, the balance of the meal has altered, offering even greater variety through smaller dishes.

My favourite *antipasto* is the *acciughe in salsa verde* – the largest anchovy fillets, with masses of finely-chopped parsley, garlic and chilli, preserved in oil. The fish are particularly piquant, good with bread and butter, and make the best midnight snack – the creak of the fridge door betrays the fact that someone in the house is hungry!

An *antipasto* always provides great variety and good-quality dishes that reflect the specialist knowledge of the chef. Try to develop some interesting new dishes for yourself, and remember to think about the culinary traditions of the particular Italian region associated with the ingredients used or the other dishes to follow – *Buon Appetito!*

Pinzimonio

CRUDITÉS WITH EXTRA-VIRGIN OLIVE OIL

2 bunches of spring onions, trimmed
4 small tender artichokes, outer leaves removed, cut into eighths
2 young fennel bulbs, cut lengthwise into eighths
inner tender stalks, plus hearts, of 4 young heads of celery
8 small new carrots
1 ramekin or small dish per person full of extra-virgin olive oil
salt and pepper
good bread, to serve

Put the vegetables in a large bowl containing ice cubes and a little water and place on the centre of the table. Add to each dish of olive oil a teaspoon of salt and a teaspoon of pepper, which will collect at the bottom.

Each guest takes a piece of vegetable, dips it in the oil while trying to collect a little of the salt and pepper, and eats it accompanied by good bread.

Pinzimonio, also called *cazzimperio* in Rome, is the pleasant surprise put on your tables as you sit down in good Tuscan trattorias.

Olive Oil

This miraculous product is made by pressing the pulp of the olive, itself the fruit of an amazing tree, native to most of the Mediterranean region. In the last 2,000 years, however, olive oil has become a symbol of Italian agricultural expertise. It is not so much the quantity, although Italy is the largest producer after Spain, but the unique characteristics that make it the best-known olive oil in the world. With the exception of Piedmont and Lombardy, where climate and soil are unsuitable, all other 18 Italian regions grow olives. most of which go towards making about 824,000 tonnes of oil, half of which is extra-virgin.

To produce this kind of quantity the trees need a great deal of care, especially as 58% of the 1,176,000 hectares devoted to them is on hilly slopes. One of the most difficult provinces for growing is Liguria, where, high in the hills, the trees have to be planted on terraces and can only be reached on foot. The Ligurian oil is one of the lightest and it is produced exclusively from one type of olive, the relatively small Taggiasca.

Fiori di Zucchini Fritti

DEEP-FRIED COURGETTE FLOWERS

Courgette Flowers

Like other plants in the squash family, courgettes have exquisite flowers which are edible. Only the non-fruit-bearing male flower, with its characteristic long thin stem, is usually sold in huge bunches at markets all around Italy. Courgette flowers are at their best when open and are ideal for stuffing with mixtures of spinach, ricotta and parmesan before being dipped in beaten egg and deep-fried. They are also good simply dipped in a batter of flour, water and salt then deep- or shallow-fried in good olive oil.

Recently, due to demand for the flowers, courgette plants have been bred expressly for their flowers and only tiny courgettes are produced as a result. These baby courgettes are extremely tender but, like all plants that are not allowed to reach maturity, lack flavour in comparison with the fully grown vegetable.

2 eggs
150 g (5 oz) plain flour
4 tbsp beer
20 courgette flowers, orange-coloured but still closed
salt and pepper
olive oil for deep-frying

Beat the eggs with some salt and pepper and then add the flour and beer and mix well to obtain a light batter. If the flowers are already open, check for insects inside.

Dip the flowers in the batter one by one and deep-fry in hot oil, a few at a time, until golden. Use a fairly small pan for frying so the oil level is higher and you will need less. Drain briefly on kitchen paper and serve as soon as possible.

There are two ways of cooking this delightful curiosity – either stuffed or simply dipped in batter and fried. Both ways are wonderful.

Sun-dried Vegetables

Drying tomatoes in the sun was one of the many inventive ways the Italians devised to ensure themselves a supply of the vital vegetable all year round. Since then sun-dried tomatoes have become as prized for their characteristic meaty flavour and texture as for their keeping qualities. Only relatively recently did the rest of the world wake up to their potential, much to the surprise of the Italians, who had been using them for centuries.

Their success has spawned a great array of similar specialities, including sun-dried aubergines, peppers and courgettes. The vegetables are cut into slices, sprinkled with salt and then laid out on trays in the sun like the tomatoes. If you want, you can get a roughly similar effect at home by putting the vegetable slices on trays in a very low oven for several hours.

Zucchini alla Scapece

MARINATED COURGETTES

800 g (1¾ lb) young courgettes, cut into slices 2 mm (1/12 inch) thick
2 tbsp mint leaves
1 garlic clove, peeled and cut in half
salt
about 2 tbsp white wine vinegar
olive oil for frying

Fry the courgette slices in abundant hot oil until browned on both sides (not too dark). The courgettes have to swim freely in the oil; if necessary, fry them in batches. Drain through a sieve to get rid of excess oil and then put them in a porcelain dish.

When all the courgettes have been fried, add the mint leaves and the garlic (which is only to flavour the courgettes and should be discarded before eating). Season with salt to taste and stir in at least 2 tablespoons of vinegar, more if desired. Leave to marinate for at least 2 hours.

Scapece probably comes from the Portuguese word *escabèche*, meaning marinated. As well as being a delightful *antipasto*, it is also makes a good accompaniment for grilled lamb or pork.

Char-grilling Vegetables

Char-grilling is most effective when done over real charcoal, because of the woody smoky flavour it gives to the food. It is a very healthy way of cooking vegetables as well as giving them added flavour. Although radicchio was one of the first vegetables to be grilled, courgettes, aubergines, peppers, onions and artichokes are also good. Just after they have been removed from the grill, the skins of vegetables, like peppers and tomatoes, peel off with ease. Harder vegetables like fennel and celeriac need to be blanched first, then cut into slices before grilling. To prevent the vegetables from getting too charred and to give them even more flavour, brush them with a marinade of olive oil, lemon, crushed garlic, salt and pepper.

Melanzane Fritte

FRIED AUBERGINES

2 large aubergines, cut into finger-sized strips
125 ml (4 fl oz) olive oil
salt

Leave the aubergine strips in lightly salted cold water for an hour, then drain and squeeze out the excess water. Heat the oil in a large pan, add the aubergines and fry until brown on each side. Season with salt to taste. They can be served hot or cold.

Peperoni Fritti

FRIED PEPPERS

6 tbsp olive oil
600 g (1¼ lb) whole baby sweet peppers
2 garlic cloves
½ small chilli, deseeded and chopped
salt

Heat the oil in a heavy pan and add the peppers. Fry for 5 minutes, stirring from time to time so that they fry on all sides. When the skins begin to blister, add the garlic and almost immediately afterwards the chilli and salt to taste. Cook for a further 5 minutes. Serve hot or cold.

Clockwise from the top left: Zucchini alla Scapece (page 15), Peperoni Fritti, Peperoni e Olive (page 18), Melanzane Fritte

Aubergine

This vegetable is common throughout the Mediterranean region and used in an infinite number of recipes. In Italy, it is mainly eaten in the South and is grown in Campania, Puglia, Calabria, Sicily and Sardinia. Aubergines may be long and oval in shape or round like a huge egg.

When fresh, they should be quite firm to the touch. They usually have rather tough skins, ranging in colour from dark purple to pale violet and even white (hence the American name eggplant). The pulp is white or slightly green, with a lot of little soft seeds. The aubergine has a slightly bitter taste, especially in the thinner varieties, so prior to cooking these are often sliced and sprinkled with salt, then left to rest while the bitter juices are drawn out. To avoid the aubergines absorbing too much oil, blanch them prior to cooking.

Perhaps the best-known recipe for aubergine in Italy is an aubergine preserve, melanzane sott'olio, *in which the aubergine is cut lengthwise into ribbons then cooked in vinegar and salt before being thoroughly drained, put into a jar mixed with dried oregano, very finely chopped garlic and pieces of chilli pepper and covered with good olive oil.*

Peperoni e Olive

PEPPERS AND OLIVES

125 ml (4 fl oz) olive oil

2 each yellow and red peppers, deseeded and cut into large strips

2 tbsp finely chopped black olives

2 garlic cloves, finely chopped

2 tbsp white wine vinegar

1 tsp sugar

salt

Heat the oil in a pan, add the peppers and fry, stirring from time to time, for about 20 minutes, until they are tender.

Add the olives and garlic and fry for another couple of minutes. Add the vinegar and stir until it has evaporated, then add the sugar and some salt to taste. Serve hot or cold.

This simple mixture of peppers and olives is a very welcome Southern addition to an *antipasto*.

Paté di Olive Nere

BLACK OLIVE PASTE

500 g (1 lb) firm black olives, stoned
25 g (¾ oz) salted capers, soaked in water for 10 minutes and then drained
4 anchovy fillets
1 tsp freshly ground black pepper
1 small chilli, chopped (optional)
pinch of fresh or dried oregano (optional)
125 ml (4 fl oz) extra-virgin olive oil

Put all the ingredients except the oil in a blender or liquidizer. With the motor running, add the oil a little at a time until you have a spreadable paste. No salt is necessary because of the olives, capers and anchovies, which are already salted. If you include the chilli, reduce the amount of black pepper.

The paste can also be made with green olives, although the anchovies should then be replaced by a handful of ground almonds.

Olive

If you were to eat an olive picked straight from the tree you would find it extremely bitter; whether ripe (black) or unripe (green), it is inedible. It is the salt-curing process that makes olives palatable.

Olives grown for consumption are generally different varieties from those grown for oil production, with the exception of the Taggiasca grown in Liguria for both. Edible olives, called 'da tavola'*, are mostly grown in the South and include varieties such as the fairly large green Ascolana in the Marche, the Pugliese Cerignola, Maiatica and Molellara, and in Sicily, the Bella di Spagna, Santa Agostino and Santa Caterina.*

Olive Ascolane

STUFFED OLIVES

55 g (1¾ oz) butter
300 g (10½ oz) each minced pork and beef
grated zest of ½ lemon
1 glass of dry white wine
1 tbsp tomato paste
100 g (3½ oz) salami, very finely chopped
55 g (1¾ oz) mortadella, very finely chopped
55 g (1¾ oz) parmesan cheese, grated
2 tbsp chopped flat-leaf parsley
5 eggs
48–50 very large green olives (preferably Ascolane olives)
salt, pepper and freshly grated nutmeg
flour and breadcrumbs for coating
olive oil for deep-frying

Heat the butter in a pan, add the meats, lemon zest and nutmeg, salt and pepper and fry for a few minutes. Stir in the white wine and tomato paste and cook gently for 30–40 minutes. Leave to cool and then stir in the salami, mortadella, parmesan, parsley and 2 of the eggs. Process in a blender to obtain a fairly soft paste that still has a little texture.

Using a very sharp curved small knife, cut the flesh of each olive from the stone in a spiral fashion to open it up in a continuous strip of peel. Stuff each olive case with a little filling, reshaping it as a large olive.

Beat the remaining eggs together. Dust the stuffed olives in flour, then coat them with beaten egg and roll in breadcrumbs. Deep-fry in batches in a small pan of oil. Drain on kitchen paper. If serving them hot, sprinkle with some lemon juice; otherwise they can be eaten cold.

Peperoni Ripieni

STUFFED PEPPERS

3 large yellow or red peppers, or a mixture of both
300 g (10½ oz) fresh breadcrumbs
1 tbsp salted capers, soaked in water for 10 minutes and then drained
1 tbsp finely chopped black olives
3 large tomatoes, peeled, deseeded and finely diced
1 garlic clove, very finely chopped
2 tbsp coarsely chopped flat-leaf parsley
4 anchovy fillets, finely chopped
125 ml (4 fl oz) olive oil
salt and pepper

Preheat the oven to 180°C/350°F/gas 4. Cut the peppers in half and discard the seeds.

Soak the breadcrumbs in enough water to cover and then squeeze out the excess liquid. Mix with the capers, olives, tomatoes, garlic, parsley, anchovies, half the olive oil and salt and pepper to taste. Fill the peppers with this mixture and put them on a baking tray. Sprinkle with the rest of the olive oil and bake for 30 minutes, until the peppers are tender and starting to char a little at the edges.

They are excellent hot or cold.

Serves 6

This way of preparing peppers is typical of the South. With a few variations, this is how they are cooked in Naples.

Capsicum

Along with the aubergine, the sweet pepper is perhaps the vegetable most closely associated with Mediterranean countries. Native to South America, the pepper was introduced to Italy towards the end of the eighteenth century, when it became a popular ingredient in Italian cooking.

The cultivation of the pepper, which takes its name from the spicy flavour similar to that of a peppercorn, is widespread throughout Italy. The squarish Quadrato di Asti is grown all over Italy, but most notably in Piedmont, where it is used in the celebrated local dip, bagna caôda. *Of the other varieties, there is the Carnoso di Cuneo, a large meaty pepper of yellow or red and sometimes green. Another variety looks like a tomato, being bright red in colour and squarish, almost squashed. My mother used to pickle this in vinegar for the winter when she would cook it with chunks of pork. Peppers may also be long and conical in shape like the lungo Marconi. The very small green peppers are good cooked whole (see page 16), although it is worth tasting one first to check the flavour.*

Frittelle di Borraggine

BORAGE FRITTERS

300 g (10½ oz) borage leaves and tops (with flowers)
100 g (3½ oz) plain flour
pinch of salt
2 eggs, beaten
a little milk
plenty of olive oil for frying

Blanch the borage in boiling salted water for 3 minutes, then drain thoroughly and leave to cool.

Sift the flour and salt into a bowl. Whisk in the eggs and enough milk to make a batter with a fairly liquid consistency. Dip a few borage leaves in the batter at a time and shallow-fry in plenty of hot olive oil until golden. Drain on paper towels.

The fritters are best served warm, but they are also good cold.

In Campania, borage is used as a vegetable, like spinach, in soups and with beans. These fritters are excellent served with *apéritifs.*

Borage

This unusual plant, with its pretty pale blue and yellow flowers (used for decorating salads and desserts) and large deep green, hairy leaves, is very popular in two Italian regions, Campania and Liguria.

I like to boil the leaves until tender, then sauté them briefly in extra-virgin olive oil, with garlic and a little chilli, and sprinkle them with lemon juice just before serving.

In Liguria, where borage grows freely with many other herbs, it is cooked in a similar way and is an essential part of preboggion, *a mixture of wild herbs used as a filling for* pansôti, *the local stuffed pasta.*

Acciughe Marinate

MARINATED ANCHOVIES

Anchovy

Probably the best-loved and most versatile of Italian fish, anchovies are small saltwater fish which live in deep waters and approach the shore only during the spring mating season. The fishing of this speciality is strictly controlled to avoid damaging stocks. Being a lovely blue-green colour, they are classified by Italians as among the pesce azzurro, *or blue fish, along with sardines and mackerel.*

The adult fish grow to a maximum of 20 cm (8 inches) in length and are either used fresh in a variety of regional dishes or preserved in salt and olive oil. At their best, these preserved anchovies have all the flavour and aroma of freshly caught fish.

Anchovies are central to the cuisine of the southern coastal regions of Italy. The best fresh acciughe *or* alici, *as they are sometimes called in the South, can be found in the Gulf of Naples.*

Fresh anchovies should be used very quickly as the delicate and fragrant flesh deteriorates quickly. The fillets can be eaten raw with just a few drops of lemon juice sprinkled over them; or marinated as here.

1 garlic clove, peeled and cut in half
juice of 2 lemons
500 g (1 lb) extremely fresh anchovies
6 tbsp olive oil
1 tbsp finely chopped flat-leaf parsley
salt and pepper
1 tomato, deseeded and diced, to garnish (optional)

Put the garlic in the lemon juice and leave for about an hour, then discard the garlic when the juice has taken on its aroma.

Meanwhile, cut the heads off the anchovies, then slit them down the belly, gut them and open them out flat. Lay them skin-side down on a non-metallic plate.

Whisk together the lemon juice, olive oil, parsley, and salt and pepper to taste. Pour this dressing over the anchovies and leave to marinate for at least a couple of hours before serving.

Sprinkle with a garnish of chopped tomato to serve, if you like.

Delicious *antipasti di mare* like these start the meal at the San Giovanni Restaurant in Casarza, Liguria.

Centre: Sardine Ripiene (page 37); clockwise from the top: Totano Ripieno (page 31), Cozze Ripiene (page 30), Pesce Spada Carpaccio (page 35), Acciughe Marinate, Insalata di Moscardini (page 33)

Mussel

One of the most common shellfish in the world, the mussel is used abundantly in Italian cuisine, especially in southern Italy and the Venetian lagoon where what they call locally peoci *are prodigious.*

In the clear waters near Chioggia in the Venetian lagoon there is farm after farm where mussels grow on long ropes hanging from wooden frames. The farms are carefully regulated to ensure high standards of hygiene because of the susceptibility of the mussel to pollution.

When bought, mussels must be firmly closed (or close when tapped) and heavy, indicating that they are still alive and so completely fresh. Before cooking, they should be well washed under cold running water, using a knife to scrape off barnacles and the beards. Mussels which come to the surface when submerged in water should be discarded, as should those that do not open after cooking.

At one time, mussels were eaten raw like oysters but today, with the risk of contamination from pollution, it is essential to cook them first. They are most commonly cooked in a little wine with pepper, parsley, garlic and sometimes chilli, or they may be sprinkled with garlic and breadcrumbs and baked.

Cozze Ripiene

STUFFED MUSSELS

1 kg (2¼ lb) large black mussels
1 tbsp olive oil
2 garlic cloves, finely chopped
black pepper
1 recipe quantity of filling from Sardine Ripiene (page 37)
1 egg, beaten
breadcrumbs for coating
olive oil for deep-frying

Clean the mussels (see left) and place them in a large pan with the olive oil and garlic. Cook with a lid on for a few minutes, shaking the pan from time to time to allow the mussels to open. When they have all opened, season with black pepper and leave to cool.

Remove the mussels from their shells and enclose each one in a little of the sardine filling. Put back in the shell and then close the shell, leaving a little filling showing. Dip the mussels in the beaten egg and then in breadcrumbs. Deep-fry in olive oil until golden, and drain briefly on kitchen paper.

When bought, mussels must be firmly closed – or close when tapped – and heavy, indicating that they are still alive and so completely fresh.

Totano Ripieno

STUFFED TOTANO SQUID

2 large squid, preferably totano, weighing about 500 g (1 lb) in total
25 g (¾ oz) butter
breadcrumbs from 2 bread rolls
a little milk
1 garlic clove, very finely chopped
25 g (¾ oz) pine nuts
1 tbsp finely chopped flat-leaf parsley
2 eggs
salt and pepper

Prepare the squid (see right) and cut off the tentacles. Chop the tentacles and fry them in the butter for 6–8 minutes, then set aside.

Soak the breadcrumbs in a little milk to cover, then squeeze out the excess liquid. Mix with the garlic, pine nuts, parsley, and salt and pepper to taste. Bind with the eggs and stir in the cooked tentacles. Stuff the squid cavities with this mixture and secure with a toothpick or sew up with a needle and kitchen string.

The squid are best steamed for about 30 minutes but you may also braise them in a pan with lard and a little butter for 20 minutes. When the squid are cooked, leave them to cool and then slice them to serve.

Squid

Squid have tube-like bodies with two fins, and a head with eight short tentacles and two longer than the others which are lined with small suckers. The differences between the many varieties of calamaro *are more to do with size and shape than taste or texture. The totano seppia, or flying squid, is notable for its habit of leaping from the water and gliding for some distance. Found mostly off Liguria, it is treated much as other squid, but has coarser flesh.*

To prepare squid for cooking, the pink-hued skin is first removed, then the transparent quill inside the tube discarded. The black ink sac inside the body should be removed carefully and reserved if you want to use it to colour a dish.

ZENGA

Insalata di Moscardini

BABY OCTOPUS SALAD

500 g (1 lb) moscardini (baby octopus, see right)
4 tbsp olive oil
1½ tbsp lemon juice
1 garlic clove, very finely chopped
1 tbsp chopped flat-leaf parsley
salt and pepper

Boil the moscardini in lightly salted water for about 12 minutes, until tender (the larger they are, the more cooking time is required).

Drain and dress with the olive oil, lemon juice, garlic, parsley and salt and pepper.

At a famous stand in Palermo's Vucceria market, freshly caught *polpo* is cooked in an old aluminium pot. Into the boiling water goes the fresh, creamy-coloured octopus and after a few minutes out it comes, extremely tender and an appetizing pinky-red. It is cut up for eating straight away with freshly squeezed lemon juice.

Octopus

The octopus, or polpo, *can be found easily on all Italian coasts and is very much prized. It has a strong beak in the centre of its oval body which, along with the eyes, has to be discarded when preparing it for cooking. It can be eaten in salads or freshly poached,* affogato, *as in Naples, or cooked in a covered pot with some oil, garlic, tomatoes, olives, chilli and parsley.*

The smaller moscardino, *which has only one row of suckers on its tentacles, is not so well appreciated in the kitchen although it is still very good. The same recipes can be used for both, reducing the cooking time for the smaller creature.*

In coastal towns, street vendors fillet anchovies, sardines and herrings straight from the boats while you wait.

Acciughe Farcite al Forno

STUFFED BAKED ANCHOVIES

24 very fresh anchovies, boned and opened butterfly-fashion
6 tbsp olive oil
2 garlic cloves, very finely chopped
4 tbsp finely chopped fresh parsley
1 tbsp finely chopped fresh basil leaves
5 sage leaves, finely chopped
1 small chilli, very finely chopped
25 g (¾ oz) pine nuts
30 g (1 oz) raisins
juice of 1 lemon
30 g (1 oz) dry breadcrumbs
salt and pepper

Preheat the oven to 220°C/425°F/gas 7 and grease a baking sheet with some of the olive oil.

In a bowl, mix the garlic, herbs, chilli, pine nuts and raisins with salt and pepper to taste. Add 1 tablespoon of the olive oil and a few drops of lemon juice and mix well.

Lay 12 of the anchovies skin side down next to each other on the prepared baking sheet. Distribute the mixture on top of them, sprinkle with a few drops of lemon juice and sandwich with the remaining anchovies, skin side up. Sprinkle with the breadcrumbs and drizzle over the remaining olive oil.

Bake for 10–12 minutes, until just starting to brown. Serve hot, sprinkled with the remaining lemon juice, or cold arranged on lemon slices.

Pesce Spada Carpaccio

SWORDFISH CARPACCIO

8 very thin slices of fresh swordfish fillet
3 tbsp olive oil
juice of 1 lemon
1 tbsp very finely chopped flat-leaf parsley
1 spring onion, chopped
1 tsp pink peppercorns, lightly crushed
salt and pepper

Lay the slices of fish on a non-metallic plate. Mix together all the remaining ingredients and season the mixture with lots of pepper. Pour this mixture over the fish and leave to marinate for 30 minutes.

True *carpaccio* is raw beef fillet, but nowadays the term is used for all manner of thinly sliced meat and fish dressed with a marinade. Raw fish has not traditionally been eaten in Italy, but it has recently become fashionable.

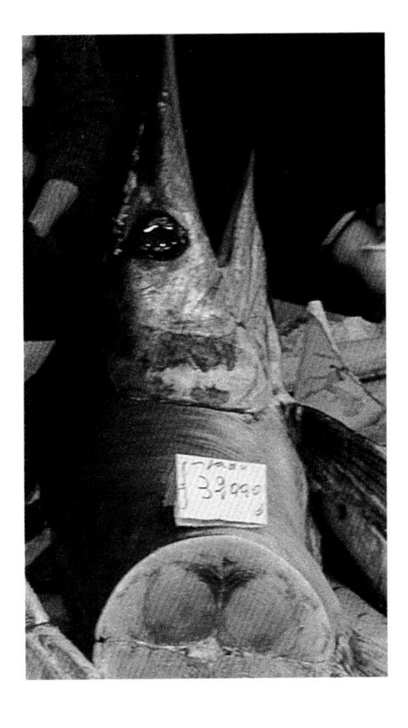

Swordfish

Swordfish reach up to 4 metres (12 ft) in length and 200 kg (450 lb) in weight. The fish is readily identified by the long sword or spear on its snout. Many are harpooned by fishermen off the coasts of Calabria and Sicily. It is one of those fish that is generally hung for at least one day before use. The flesh is very similar in texture, colour and taste to that of shark meat and for this reason is cut and cooked in a similar way. It is mostly grilled but more recently it has been served raw as carpaccio *and smoked.*

Sardine alla Beccafico

ROLLED BAKED SARDINES

2 tbsp extra-virgin olive oil
125 g (4½ oz) dry breadcrumbs
2 tbsp soft raisins (soaked beforehand if necessary)
2 tbsp pine nuts
juice of 2 large oranges
salt and pepper
16 very fresh sardines, heads removed, butterflied open and backbone removed
18 fresh bay leaves

In a frying pan, heat the olive oil and fry the breadcrumbs gently, stirring with a wooden spoon, until toasted and brown. Allow to cool.

Preheat the oven to 200°C/400°F/gas 6.

Add the raisins, pine nuts, the juice of 1 of the oranges, salt and abundant pepper to the fried breadcrumbs. Mix well.

Wash the sardines and pat dry with kitchen towel. Arrange them skin side down. Place a spoonful of the filling on each of the sardines and roll them up. Arrange tightly together on a baking tray, placing bay leaves between them, and bake for 20 minutes.

As soon as the sardines come out of the oven, sprinkle them with the juice of the remaining orange.

Sardine Ripiene

STUFFED SARDINES

12 very fresh large sardines
1 egg, beaten
breadcrumbs for coating
olive oil for deep-frying
FOR THE FILLING:
breadcrumbs from 2 bread rolls
a little milk
60 g (2 oz) extremely fresh mortadella, diced
2 eggs
55 g (1¾ oz) parmesan cheese, grated
1 garlic clove, very finely chopped
2 tbsp finely chopped flat-leaf parsley
salt and pepper

Cut the heads off the sardines and bone them, leaving them attached down the back.

Prepare the filling: soak the breadcrumbs in a little milk to cover, then squeeze out excess liquid. Mix with the remaining filling ingredients and season. Use to stuff the sardines, then close each sardine like a sandwich. Dip in the beaten egg and then in breadcrumbs. Deep-fry in olive oil until golden, drain briefly on kitchen paper and serve.

Venice's wonderful fish market at the Rialto.

Sardine

The name of this fish, actually young pilchard, probably comes from the area where it was mostly fished and known to the Romans around the Island of Sardinia. It is eaten in most of the Mediterranean countries and is almost a staple of all the coastal areas of Italy, where it is not only consumed fresh but also preserved in oil and in salt like the anchovy. The flesh is relatively fatty and the best way to eat sardines is brushed with a little lemon juice, olive oil, parsley, garlic, salt and pepper and then grilled. They can also be boned and stuffed or dipped in flour, egg and breadcrumbs and deep-fried.

The Sicilians honour the sardine in two special ways; firstly using it as a sauce for pasta con le sarde *and secondly as Sardine alla Beccafico* *(see page 36).*

Left: Acciughe Farcite al Forno (page 34);
Right: Sardine alla Beccafico (page 36).

Salsa Verde

GREEN SAUCE

6 salted anchovy fillets, soaked in water for 10 minutes and then drained
25 g (¾ oz) salted capers, soaked in water for 10 minutes and then drained
2 garlic cloves
large bunch of flat-leaf parsley
4 basil leaves
extra-virgin olive oil

Chop the anchovies, capers, garlic, parsley and basil very finely with a knife (not in a food processor). Stir in enough olive oil to make a very dense sauce.

Serve the *salsa verde* with bread or *grissini* and some fresh creamy unsalted butter.

At the Trattoria Italia in Castelletto Stura, Piedmont, this unusual *salsa verde* is put on each table regardless of whether or not it has been ordered. A huge bowl of impeccably cleaned vegetables is also presented to your table with a knife so you can prepare your own salad!

SALSICCIA DI FEGATO
SALSICCIA DI CERVO
SALAME AL TARTUFO TUBER AESTIVUM
CIAUSCO
SALSICCIA DI CINGHIALE AL TARTUFO
SALSICCIA DI CINGHIALE

PANE COTTO CON
FORNO A LEGNA

PROSCIUTTO
TIPICO
UMBRO

SALAME
DI PROSCIUTTO
TASCABILE

Coioni
di
Mulo

PANE CON OLIVE
PANE CON NOCI
PANE CON FORMAGGIO
PANE DELLA NONNA

ALUMI
IPICI
I MAIALE

Caponnet

SAVOY CABBAGE PARCELS

8 Savoy cabbage leaves (see below)
100 g (3½ oz) fresh pork sausages, preferably luganiga
200 g (7 oz) left-over roast meat, finely minced
2 eggs, beaten
2 tbsp dried breadcrumbs
1 garlic clove, very finely chopped
pinch of freshly grated nutmeg
55 g (1¾ oz) parmesan cheese, grated
25 g (¾ oz) butter
salt and pepper

Preheat the oven to 160°C/325°F/gas 3. Boil the cabbage leaves in lightly salted water for 5 minutes, until they are flexible. Drain and pat dry on a cloth. Cut out the central stalk if it is tough.

Take the sausage meat out of its skin and crumble it. Mix with the roast meat, eggs, breadcrumbs, garlic, nutmeg and 45 g (1½ oz) of the cheese. Season. Place the mixture in the centre of the cabbage leaves and fold them up to make parcels, securing with a cocktail stick.

Put them on a baking tray, dot with the butter and dust with the remaining parmesan. Bake for 20 minutes. Serve hot or cold.

Use the second layer of cabbage leaves as the outer layer will be too tough. In Ivrea, this dish is a must at winter parties and celebrations.

Cabbage

An old Italian saying 'come il cavolo a merenda' *translates 'as cabbage for tea', meaning something completely out of place or without sense. I would be very offended if I were a cabbage, because this underrated vegetable is one of the foundations of modern Italian cuisine and is as popular in the South as the North.*

The cabbage helped us to get through the War and I remember eating it disguised in many ways by my mother who was keen to give us satisfying and nutritious food. She cooked it in lots of imaginative ways, using various types of cabbage. Her unforgettable cooking has been such a great inspiration in my professional life.

Piedmont, Lombardy and the Veneto make particular use of the cavolo verza *(Savoy cabbage), distinguished by its wrinkled and curly leaves. The deep green, almost blue, outer leaves are often wrapped around a meat stuffing, as here. The paler internal leaves are very tender and make a wonderful salad if their thick ribs are removed. The leaves are then finely shredded and dressed with an anchovy vinaigrette.*

Cipolle Ripiene

STUFFED ONIONS

8 large onions (the size of a small orange)
200 g (7 oz) fresh pork sausages, preferably luganiga
1 tbsp olive oil
1 tbsp breadcrumbs
1 egg, beaten
1 tbsp raisins
1 tbsp pine nuts
2 amaretti biscuits, crumbled
1 tbsp parmesan cheese, grated
small pinch of freshly grated nutmeg
pinch of cinnamon
salt and pepper

Preheat the oven to 180°C/350°F/gas 4. Peel the onions. Cook them in lightly salted boiling water for 10 minutes and then drain.

Take the sausage meat out of its skin and crumble it. Heat the olive oil in a frying pan, add the sausage meat and fry until browned. Leave to cool, then mix with the breadcrumbs, beaten egg, raisins, pine nuts, crumbled amaretti biscuits, cheese, nutmeg and cinnamon, adding salt and pepper to taste.

Cut the top off each onion and remove the centre with a spoon to make a container. Fill them with the stuffing and bake for 20–25 minutes. They can be served hot or cold.

Onion

The onion has been used for thousands of years in Italy. Introduced by the Egyptians then taken up by the Romans, it has been put to use in all sorts of ways, including being fermented to make an alcoholic drink. In the Italian kitchen it is widely used in ragùs, soups and risottos. The main areas of cultivation are Sicily, Puglia, Campania and Emilia-Romagna.

The onion has been cultivated through the centuries to produce thousands of varieties, with all manner of shapes, colours and strengths. Most are named after cities, such as Ramata di Milano and Rossa Piatta di Bassano, but there are far too many to list here.

The pink-and-golden-coloured onions have the most intense flavour, while the white and red are usually milder. The best red onions are those from Tropea in Calabria, celebrated for their sweetness.

I have two tips to help overcome the worst effects of onions when preparing them: first to stop them from making you cry, soak them in water for 30 minutes before handling them and breathe through your mouth rather than your nose when you cut them; secondly, to get rid of the smell of onions on your fingers, rub them with salt.

Carne all'Albese

ALBA-STYLE RAW BEEF WITH PARMESAN AND WHITE TRUFFLE

400 g (14 oz) beef fillet, cut into very thin slices
4 tbsp extra-virgin olive oil
juice of 1 lemon
4 celery stalks, thinly sliced
12 fresh asparagus tips, cooked until just al dente
85 g (3 oz) parmesan cheese, thinly sliced
45 g (1½ oz) white truffle, cut into thin shavings
salt and pepper

Put the slices of beef between 2 sheets of heavy-duty cling film and beat gently with a meat mallet or the end of a rolling pin until very thin. It should be about 1–2 mm (1/16 inch) thick.

Spread the meat over 4 large serving plates without letting the slices overlap. Season with salt and pepper, then brush with the olive oil and lemon juice. Distribute the slices of celery, asparagus tips, parmesan and white truffle over the meat and serve with *grissini*.

The attraction of this sophisticated dish from Piedmont lies in its simplicity and, naturally, in the unbeatable combination of the meat with truffles.

Carpaccio

This similar dish of very thin slices of raw beef, dressed with a sauce based on mustard, ketchup and other spices, was made for the first time in the legendary Harry's Bar in Venice. The term carpaccio *is now used all over the culinary world to indicate very thinly cut food – meat, fish or even vegetables – dressed with a marinating sauce, usually based on lemon juice or vinegar, oil and spices.*

Affettato

This term covers all preserved meats, but is mostly used for pork products like prosciutto and salami. However, items as varied as bresaola *and wild boar may be included.*

Affettato Misto

PIEDMONTESE SLICED MEAT ANTIPASTO

8 thin slices of prosciutto crudo
4 thin slices of coppa
4 thin slices of mortadella
8 slices of salami
about 12 sweet-and-sour pickled onions
85 g (3 oz) preserved wild mushrooms
4 artichoke hearts in oil, drained
85 g (3 oz) mixed pickles
Zucchini alla Scapece (page 15)
good country bread and/or *grissini*

Just before you want to serve the *antipasto*, arrange the sliced meats attractively on a large serving platter. Put the pickles and vegetables in separate bowls and scatter these around the table for people to help themselves.

Serve with good country bread and/or *grissini*.

The *antipasto* of *affettato misto* is so beloved by many Italians. *Prosciutto crudo* is the essential ingredient in an Italian *antipasto* and the various pickles balance the fat content of the preserved meats.

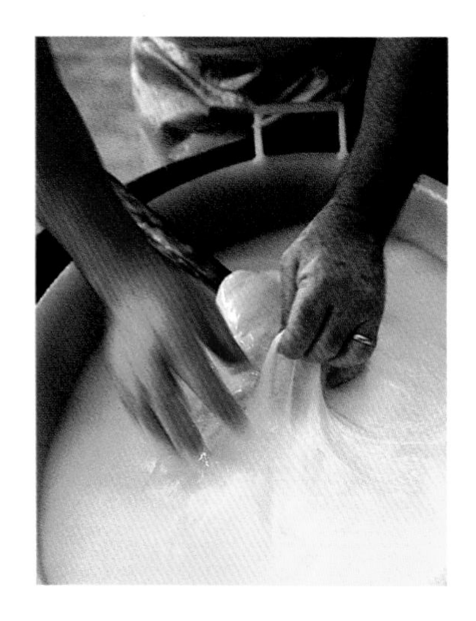

Mozzarella in Carrozza

FRIED MOZZARELLA SANDWICH

2 thick slices of pane di campagna (country-style white bread)
milk
1 large slice of buffalo mozzarella
salt
flour for dusting
2 eggs, beaten
olive oil for frying

Dip the slices of bread in milk for a few seconds but do not soak them. Drain, then place the mozzarella on one piece of bread and put the other on top to make a sandwich. Dip in flour seasoned with salt, then the egg. Shallow-fry in a good quantity of oil for 5 minutes until golden, turning once. Serve immediately.
For 1

Originally from Naples and generally from Campania, this dish has spread all over Italy and is to be found mostly in bars as a lunch-time snack. It is delicious when freshly made and still crisp.

Mozzarella Cheese

*This southern Italian cheese is named after the technique of tearing apart or cutting (*mozzata*) the whey with the fingers to form balls of cheese. It is mainly produced in Battipaglia in the province of Salerno, but is also made in Caserta and the provinces of Naples, Puglia and Lazio. Authentic buffalo-milk cheese is traditionally produced by only a few specialists, as there is not enough buffalo milk to meet the demands of commercial production.*

What makes mozzarella so special is its unusually low fat content. The richness of the buffalo milk, with only 7 to 7.5% fat, also gives it its distinctive taste. The cheese has been made since the thirteenth century – the same techniques are still used today.

Bruschetta

ITALIAN SAVOURY TOAST

1 loaf of ciabatta bread, cut into slices 5 cm (2 inches) thick
2 large garlic cloves, peeled
8 tbsp extra-virgin olive oil
2 large ripe beef tomatoes, very finely chopped
6 basil leaves
salt and pepper

Preheat the oven to 200°C/400°F/gas 6 and bake the bread for 10–15 minutes until golden. Rub the garlic over the hot bread. Drizzle half the oil over it, then sprinkle the tomatoes on top and add a basil leaf. Season and drizzle over the rest of the oil. Serve warm or cold.
Makes 6

Bruschetta

Bruschetta *is a slice of toasted bread flavoured with oil, fats or garlic, to be eaten on its own as a snack or served with* antipasto. *The most common way of serving* bruschetta *is brushed with a clove of garlic and drizzled with a little extra-virgin olive oil. Another method is to spread the toast with good-quality pork lard or goose fat. In Lazio and Abruzzi, olive oil is drizzled over and a little chopped tomato and basil added. In Tuscany,* bruschetta *is called* fettunta *or* panunto, *meaning 'greased slice of bread' and it is usually made with an unsalted bread called* pane sciocco.

The 'improved' bruschetta *shown here makes a hearty snack or even a good light meal.*

Fettunta

TUSCAN TOASTED BREAD

8 slices of Tuscan country-style unsalted bread
1 garlic clove, peeled
6 tbsp Tuscan extra-virgin olive oil
salt and pepper

Toast the bread on both sides, then gently rub with the garlic. Drizzle over the olive oil, sprinkle with salt and pepper and eat warm.
Makes 8

Glossary of Antipasto Ingredients

***Bresaola** / Air-dried Beef*
The Valtellina Valley in Lombardy has a long tradition of curing and air-drying beef which is then thinly cut and sprinkled with lemon juice and oil at the last minute for serving as an *antipasto*. Round in shape and only lightly salted, *bresaola* is not dissimilar to the Swiss *Bündner-fleisch*. It may have been invented to provide a source of protein when fresh meat was scarce.

***Ciabatta** / Bread*
One of the most popular breads in Italy and around the world, *ciabatta* is made with type 0 wheat flour and is characterized by its softness and moisture, both of which are due to the long raising time of 6 hours, when the large air holes are formed. Its soft crust is the result of cooking the bread in ovens where water is allowed to evaporate as the bread cooks.

***Coppa** / Neck End of Pork*
Fresh neck of pork is very juicy if braised or slowly roasted. The neck of pork is, however, often cured in salt brine, stuffed in a gut casing, bound and set to air-dry for at least 6 months to make the cured meat known as *coppa*. Due to its composition of large pieces of fat and lean meat, *coppa* looks much like a very fatty sausage. However, it is in fact only 40 per cent fat, less than other meat preserves. It is eaten thinly sliced as *antipasto*.

***Crespone** / Pure Pork Salami*
This fairly large salami is made only with pork. It is mostly available in the north of Italy and takes its name from the skin of the intestine of the pig. It is usually eaten sliced as part of an *antipasto*. See Salame.

***Crostini di Pane** / Tuscan Toasted Bread*
Crostini have recently become very fashionable all over the world. Originally from Tuscany, they are made with slices of unsalted Tuscan bread that is toasted and spread with a pâté of chicken livers, a wild boar *ragù* or vegetables. Tuscans eat this canapé with aperitifs, but selections with various toppings are now also served as a first course. The finest *crostini* are spread with a pâté and topped with a slice of truffle.

***Culatello** / Ham*
Zibello, a town near Modena, is the centre for the manufacture of this famous Emilia-Romagna ham. *Culatello* is the heart of the ham, the most tender part, cut in a round, cured in brine and enclosed in a gut-like skin before being left to air-dry for a long time. It tastes very sweet and, if correctly prepared, melts in the mouth. To enhance the taste of this delicacy further, the air-dried ham can be stripped of its skin then soaked in red wine to moisten it and add flavour. Soaked or unsoaked, this very special ham is usually served thinly sliced as part of an *antipasto* or by itself.

***Focaccia** / Flat Bread*
Focaccia is also known as *pinza* in Veneto, *pitta* in Calabria, *pizza* in Naples, *pissalandrea* in Genova, *schiacciata* in Emilia-Romagna, *fitascetta* in Lombardy, *sardenaria* in Liguria, and *stiacciata* in Tuscany. Whatever it is called, however, this bread has the same basic characteristics, being a flat bread made with a bread dough mixed with olive oil and salt. A simple version of *focaccia* was eaten by the Romans and over the centuries has developed until now there is a multitude of varieties, both salted and sweet, depending on taste and the availability of local ingredients.

Before it is cooked, the dough is pressed flat in the tin and little indentations are made with the fingers so that the olive oil that is drizzled abundantly over the dough collects in them to give the dough a wonderful flavour. Coarse salt is then sprinkled sparingly on top and the dough baked until it is golden brown.

Focaccia is eaten on its own as a snack and used to make sandwiches, when it is particularly good filled with mortadella. *Focaccia* has given rise to the pizza in Naples and the savoury and sweet version of pizza, *pinza*, in Veneto and Emilia-Romagna, using polenta flour to make the dough.

There are a huge number of different varieties of *focaccia*, including the *smacafam* from Trentino, a type of *focaccia* using buckwheat flour. The dough has onions in it and is topped with sausage meat and baked in a larded baking tray. The Calabrian *pitta* is similar to the Middle-Eastern bread, except that it is formed into a ring, cut open and filled, while still hot, with *ciccioli* (pork fat), oil and chilli or grated pecorino.

Perhaps the tastiest version of them all is the *focaccia al formaggio*, a speciality of Camogli, an enchanting fishermen's town near Genova. Two very thin layers of dough made of plain flour, water, oil and yeast, are worked in a similar way to strudel dough. The layers are filled with plenty of stracchino cheese, drizzled with olive oil and baked until the cheese has melted.

Grissino **/** *Breadstick*

Grissini, crisp thin breadsticks made using type 0 flour, water, yeast and sometimes a little olive oil, originally came from Turin but are now eaten all over the world. The long sticks of bread can reach up to 70 cm (28 inches) in length and are still handmade by stretching a piece of dough until it is round and thin before baking it until crispy and dry. To achieve an even more crumbly texture, oil or butter are added to the dough. They are also commercially made and those wrapped in cellophane can keep for many months. *Grissini* can be eaten with any food, but are mostly served with *antipasti*, or as a substitute for normal bread during a meal. They can also be wrapped in a thin slice of Parma ham to make a delicious snack.

Oliva **/** *Olive*

Olives are cured by fermentation, which usually takes place naturally courtesy of the micro-organisms in the skin, called lactic bacteria, preserving the olive from decay. The oldest method of preserving small green olives is by soaking them in water for ten days, changing the water daily, and then preserving them in salt water and storing them in a cool place. Larger olives, such as the Ascolana and Cerignola, are treated with caustic soda and lime before they are preserved in brine to sweeten them.

A Sicilian olive called Olive Bianche goes through a prolonged curing process with a very strong salt solution which leaches the colour from the olives. They are then repeatedly washed to clean away all the salt and stored in a light brine. Commercial producers of olives pasteurize, or even sterilize, them before selling them cheaply in large cans. Olives are sold in this way either whole, stoned or stuffed with peppers or pimentos. Black Baresane olives are also sweetened with caustic soda and lime, before being sterilized and canned.

Famous for its sharpness and very widely used in Italian cooking is the *oliva di gaeta*, a black olive cured in water for one day and in salt for another day, then soaked in water for 40 days and finally kept in a boiled mild brine. These olives are excellent for *antipasto*. One of my favourite olives is the small black cured variety which are baked (or dried in the oven) for a more concentrated flavour.

Italian markets sell a huge range of olives, sometimes more than 20 different varieties, whole and stuffed. Most are eaten with bread as part of an *antipasto*, but some are only suitable for cooking in one of the countless Italian recipes employing olives, especially those from Sicily where the olive is an indispensable ingredient in famous dishes such as Caponata.

Pancetta **/** *Streaky Bacon*

A very important ingredient in the preparation of many Italian dishes, pancetta is bacon cured from belly of pork, or *pancia*. Pancetta is usually fried as a base for sauces, the best known of which is *carbonara*, a sauce for pasta based on small cubes of fried pancetta – or *guanciale* as the purist requires – with the addition of raw egg at the end.

Fresh pancetta can be used to make minestrone and soups. *Pancetta curata*, salt-cured, air-dried or even *arrotolata*, rolled pancetta, is used thinly sliced as part of an *antipasto*. Today you can also find *pancetta affumicata*, smoked pancetta, which is used in many Northern Italian dishes influenced by the cuisine of neighbouring Austria. Tuscany also produces *rigatino pancetta*, 'streaky bacon', a very thin bacon that has the same uses as other pancettas.

Pane* / *Bread

One of the basic elements of the Italian diet is bread. Italians eat a great deal of bread on a daily basis, of all types and shapes according to the regional resources of grain and the type of food with which it is to be eaten.

The most common flour used for breadmaking in Italy is wheat, which is milled to make a very fine white flour. The flour is graded as 00 (*doppio zero*) and is also used to make, among other things, fresh egg pasta. Slightly less refined flour is graded 0, and so on until wholemeal flour, called *integrale*, containing the husk of the grain. It is, of course, well known that wholemeal flour is more nutritious and is a better source of roughage than white flour, but white flour and white bread are still more popular than the brown in Italy. In southern Italy, 00 (*doppio zero*) flour is mixed with durum wheat semolina to give the bread a much more solid consistency than the more delicate bread made in other parts of Italy. There are many other flours used to make bread, each of which gives a special quality to the finished product. Other flours used to make bread in Italy include rye, maize and cornflour, which is mixed with white flour for a more developed taste and more digestible bread.

The North prefers very white bread and mostly in small shapes. Liguria prefers *focaccia*, Emilia-Romagna *pane a pasta dura*, a type of white bread with a hard consistency, and a flat bread called *piadina*. Tuscany has a saltless bread called *pane sciocco*, to accompany its various savoury dishes, salami and spicy preserves. Rome loves the *sfilatino*, a short baguette also called *bastone*, or 'stick'. The entire South is definitely much happier with more substantial bread, like the *pugliese*, which is made of hard durum wheat and keeps fresh for a longer period of time.

Special breads are also made using a wide variety of flavouring ingredients, including lard, butter, olive oil, sun-dried tomatoes, herbs, olives, nuts, and a whole range of seeds.

Because it has to be fresh, bread is mostly bought on a daily basis. This is true especially in the North, because white bread rolls don't keep for more than a day. There are, however, various recipes containing stale bread which is turned into soups, salads and other specialities.

Pane a Cassetta, Pan Carré* / *Sandwich Bread

This white bread, made from type 0 flour, water and yeast, is baked in a special mould called a *cassetta*, which keeps the bread compact and dense, limiting the amount it can rise when baked and thus giving it an even square shape and thin crust. This means that, after the crust has been removed, it can be cut into smaller squares and stamped into circles to make *tartines*, canapés and sandwiches, or cut into small cubes and fried to make croutons for salads and soups.

Prosciutto* / *Cured Ham

In the past, meat had to be preserved so that it kept for a long time without the benefit of refrigeration. This need gave birth to a vast industry given over to the production of hams enjoyed as specialities in their own right rather than simply as preserved meat. Prosciutto, probably from the Latin *perexutus* meaning dried, is among the most renowned and is probably one of the best-loved foods from Italy worldwide. *Prosciutto crudo* is the essential ingredient in an Italian antipasto. It is eaten accompanied by either melon or figs and with *grissini* or good bread. It can also form part of a main course, served for example with buttered asparagus and boiled potatoes.

Parma ham, just one of the types of prosciutto produced in Italy, is so well known that any Italian ham is almost exclusively associated with it, although many other regions produce their own local hams. Parma ham is made from pigs raised in Emilia-Romagna or Lombardy, where the raw weight of the ham has to be at least 10–11 kg (22–24 lb). The production of Parma ham is controlled by the local producers' association and guarantees that the ham is locally cured and dried in the traditional way. It is also a guarantee that the pigs from which the hams are made are raised traditionally, and fed on the whey used to make Parmigiano Reggiano cheese, maize and other natural food so that the meat is tender and full of flavour. Other good local hams include the slightly smaller but very sweet-flavoured San Daniele from Friuli.

Other regions which produce good hams are Tuscany, Veneto, Campania, in the towns of Langhirano and San Leo (where, it is said, the pigs are partly fed on acorns). The best hams are cured for anything from 16 to 18 and up to 24 months. Those are cured on the bone and cut as thinly as possible by hand.

To make hams suitable for slicing by machine the bone is removed from an aged ham with a special tool by a specially trained norcino. The ham is then pressed in a mould to reshape it and vacuum-packed in heavy plastic film once it is turned out. However, the best ham is sold freshly sliced, as those sold ready-packed have little resemblance to the real thing.

According to the Association of Parma Ham Producers, during the curing process much of the saturated fat in the ham turns into unsaturated, so that prosciutto is actually a much healthier food than it might at first seem, with its perfect balance of proteins, fats, low cholesterol and an abundance of vitamins and trace elements.

Prosciutto Cotto / *Cooked Ham*

This is a variation on *prosciutto crudo* using the same cut of meat. The seasoned meat is pickled and pressed in a square-shaped mould before being steam-baked in special ovens. Like cured ham, *prosciutto cotto* is eaten as part of an *antipasto*, as well as being used for flavouring sauces and cooked vegetables or stuffings. A cheaper version is made from shoulder of pork. In some parts of Northern Italy, *prosciutto cotto* is known as *giambone*.

Salame / *Cured Sausage*

Like many preserved meats, *salame* is known as *insaccato* or 'bagged goods'. Over many years, various methods have been developed for preserving meat, including air- or sun-drying, or using salt, sugar, honey, vinegar or alcohol. Preserving meat, especially that of the annually butchered pig, has given rise to specialities like ham and sausages as well as a variety of other commodities which Italians have incorporated into their diet. As well as having an exquisite flavour, compared to a slice of plain cooked meat, good salami is highly nutritious and has the benefit of being ready to eat at any time.

The meat for salami is usually seasoned with spices which also help to preserve the meat, and it is then forced into the skins and cured.

Salami is made up of about 40 per cent fat in the form of lard or hard fat cut into cubes of different sizes, as softer fat has a tendency to turn rancid. This fat starts out highly saturated, but during the curing process much of this turns into unsaturated fat.

The meat used for salami is predominantly pork, although some salamis contain a mixture of pork and beef – or sometimes even horse meat – and the label always indicates whether it contains pure pork (*puro suino*) or pork and beef (*suino e bovino*) etc. The meat is minced to different textures and fineness depending on the type of salami being made. Additional flavourings of garlic, salt, peppercorns, chilli, fennel seed, wine, Marsala and even brandy are added. After it has been forced into the gut and moulded to the traditional shape, it is tied with string and hung in specially constructed curing rooms where the sausages are left for at least 2 to 4 months to cure under carefully controlled conditions. When the *salumi* are sold they are fully matured and will have lost at least 35 per cent of their initial weight.

In every town in every region there is a salami specialist and each one has its own local variation. Some of these salamis are now made on a large scale and sold throughout the world. The following are just a few of the many that can be found in Italy. The first group use finely minced meat, and are sometimes referred to generically as '*milano*' or '*ungherese*'.

Salame milano, also called *crespone*, is made with very finely minced pork spiced with salt, saltpetre, coarsely milled black pepper and, in some cases, crushed garlic marinated in red wine. The minced meat is forced into a natural gut to make a sausage with a diameter of about 8 cm (3¼ inches). Once bound, it is aged for at least 3 months. It is served very thinly cut.

Salame ungherese, or Hungarian salami, has been adopted by Italians who enjoy its smoky flavour. The finely minced meat is made up of equal parts pork, beef and pork fat. It is aged for at least three months and weighs around 1.5 kg (3¼ lb) when cured. It has a diameter of 6–7 cm (2½–2¾ inches) and is served very thinly sliced.

Cacciatori, or hunter's salami, is small, weighing only about 100 g (3½ oz) and only needs to be aged for a short period. It gets its name from its size, which made it convenient for hunters to carry.

The meat of the following salami is of a medium coarseness so that little chunks of meat and fat can be clearly distinguished. They are called *nostrani*.

Salame varzi, from the area of Pavia in Lombardy, is an excellent pure pork salami with 30 per cent fat. Only salt, saltpetre, whole black peppercorns and wine are added. It is about 6–7 cm (2½–2¾ inches) in diameter and is aged for 3–4 months.

Salame di felino comes from a little town near Parma and is probably one of the best Italian salamis. It is traditionally very sweet in taste and the meat used includes trimmings from the leg of pork used in making Parma ham as well as some shoulder meat. The spices added are salt, whole black peppercorns, saltpetre and perhaps some garlic and wine. Because of the type of gut used as a casing, it has a long and irregular shape, with a smaller diameter at the top than at the bottom. It takes at least three months to cure.

Salame fabriano, *salame genovese* and *salame veronese* are all very similar to the *salame di felino*, containing only a few different spices and a slightly different ratio of meat to fat.

Salame toscano or *finocchiona* or *sbriciolona*, unlike the previous salamis, contains equal amounts of pork and fat. It is also much larger, with a diameter of about 15 cm (6 inches) and tends to crumble when cut, which is why it is called *sbriciolona* ('crumbly'). The name *finocchiona* was given to it because, as well as the usual flavourings, fennel is also added.

Salame napoli is a very popular salami made up of equal parts pork, pork fat and beef. It also contains garlic, pepper, wine, salt, saltpetre, paprika and chilli, making it ideal for those who prefer a spicier flavour.

Other spicy or hot salamis include the excellent *salsiccie* made in Calabria (*salsiccia calabrese* and *napoletana*). Both are made in the same way, with the meat being pressed into a small round gut and tied into a circle.

The *soppressata* is a sort of pressed salami available all over Italy. The Venetian one, called *soppressa*, is made with pork and has a fat content of 30 per cent. It is cured for 10–15 months. The Calabrian *soppressata* is probably the most sought-after and is made up of three-quarters pork and one-quarter pork fat, cut quite coarsely with a knife and mixed with garlic, pepper, blood, paprika, wine, salt, pepper and chilli. It is smoked and cured for 3–4 months.

Speck* / *Smoked Ham Shoulder

This Austrian speciality was introduced into Italy fairly recently, previously being known only to those who lived on the border. Speck is a smoked, salt-cured, air-dried ham. It is extremely delicious on its own, but is widely used in sauces, ragùs and stews. It is similar to, but much cheaper than, Parma ham and many people eat it as an alternative as part of their *antipasto*.

Index

Publishing Director: Anne Furniss
Creative Director: Mary Evans
Editor: Lewis Esson
Consultant Art Director: Helen Lewis
Design: Sue Storey
Assistant Editor: Jane Middleton
Editorial Assistant: Rhian Bromage
Production: Candida Jackson & Vincent Smith

This edition published in 1999 by Quadrille Publishing Limited, Alhambra House, 27-31 Charing Cross Road, London WC2H OLS

Based on material originally published in *Carluccio's Complete Italian Food.*

Cataloguing-in-Publication Data: a catalogue record for this book is available from the British Library.

ISBN 1 899988 59 9

Printed and bound in Hong Kong.